Haute DOG

Haute DOG
canine couture

photography by Karen Ngo

WILLOW CREEK PRESS

Published by Willow Creek Press
P.O. Box 147, Minocqua, Wisconsin 54548

Text by Andrea Donner
Editor/design: Andrea Donner

ISBN-10: 1-59543-440-2
ISBN-13: 978-1-59543-440-1

Printed in Italy

If you look good and dress well,
you don't need a purpose in life.

—Robert Pante

CONTENTS

What's new in COLLARS

The basic collar has come a long way! There's never been a more exciting time to be a pooch than now. Collars today are available in every style to fit every occasion and personality. "Collar" sounds so restrictive—it's neckware, baby!

Fun, casual, full of personality—it's you!
For everyday wear and tear, polka dots on
durable nylon make ideal neckware.

stripes

Multi-colored stripes match any outfit or are eye-catching enough to wear alone as an accessory that stands out.

Timeless tweed is unmatched for quality and class. If you're heading out the door and need a quick collar fix that can go anywhere, reach for the tweed.

tweed

For your softer side, this pale spring floral is just the touch needed to add a pretty sparkle to your day.

A quick and easy trick to adding elegance for any formal occasion is to wear a satin sash. This one is even more opulent with gold detailing and a loosely-tied ribbon.

satin

The doggy sweater is no longer something knit by grandmas out of leftover yarn scraps! Today's ultra chic knits are colorful, comfortable, and a must-have for any dog with a sense of style.

VOGUE DOGGY SWEATERS

striped style

Perfect for weekend
romps, super comfortable
is the trademark of this
striped knit. The playful
contrasting colors
are both casual
and trendy.

wooly & warm

Want to show your skin how much you love it? Then wrap it up in this soft yellow beauty! Traditional patterns of the Scottish Isles make this sweater a classic.

fisherman's sweater

An absolute must-have for anyone living in the cold northern climes. The hand-knit quality and luxurious wool yarn are simple yet sumptuous.

classic crochet

Achieve a unique look with a crocheted sweater in pretty pinks and creams. Scalloped edging on the bottom hem makes this sweater an easy fit.

for the boys

Men wear sweaters too! Bold
navy and kelly green are a great
combination for traditional men's
styles. Simple stripes, strong
patterns, and cotton fabrics are
all sure to please those boys
who don't want to admit they
care about their clothes.

The City Girl

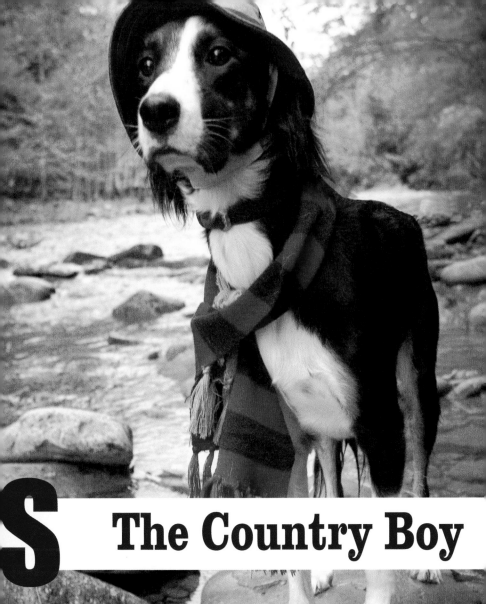

S The Country Boy

Urban girls are used to late nights out, dressing up, causing trouble, sleeping late, and doing it all over again the next night...

Looking sharp in a bright lime green crocheted scarf, this solitary country boy is up at the crack of dawn to stretch his legs and sniff what's on the wind...

This city girl is dressed to the nines in a simple pink turtle-neck with rich wool overcoat. The black striped ribbons and embellished buckle make this the perfect outfit for an evening garden party...

Equally sophisticated in earthy striped tones with matching wool scarf, this gentleman is ready for a walk down a country lane.

She's ready for another night out with this sparkly jersey knit just right for dancing. The bejeweled collar with heart pendant makes the difference between plain and absolutely fabulous...

A girl should be two things:
classy and fabulous.

—Coco Channel

He's masculine, distinguished, and warm in this elegant forest and moss green overcoat. The red stitching on the buttons adds punch that is picked up in the traditional scarf.

There has been a change in men's attitudes toward their clothes. Men are more aware of fashion; they're not afraid of it.

—Calvin Klein

Another party for her; another walk in the woods for him. She's stunning in this pale teal silk dress with ribbon and feather details, while he's the picture of down-home charm wrapped up in his simple hand-knit striped scarf.

Is your country boy ready to tie the knot?

And more importantly, are YOU marriage material?
Take the quiz and find out!

1) Thinking about being married makes you feel:
- A) Ecstatic; like running & jumping around
- B) Interested; your ears perk up a little
- C) Sick to your stomach; you feel the need to eat some grass

2) Your perfect Friday night is spent:
- A) Chasing after neighborhood dogs
- B) Sharing a bone with a good friend, male or female
- C) Partying with the bitches only

3) Watching a pack of dogs play in the park makes you:
- A) Feel like chasing your tail
- B) Feel like digging a hole
- C) Feel like running away

4) When you think about your wedding you:
- A) Fantasize about how pretty you'll look walking down the aisle
- B) Worry about having enough kibble for your guests at the reception
- C) Wonder if that door behind the altar leads outside

5) You talk about weddings with your boyfriend:
- A) On your first walk
- B) Only when he's restrained with a leash
- C) Only when you're restrained with a leash

6) Typically, your man makes you:
- A) Howl
- B) Whine
- C) Growl

Score 3 points for every "A" answer; 2 points for every "B" answer; and 1 point for every "C" answer.

12-18 points: The wedding bells are ringing already! Not only are you ready to wed, you've been planning the big day since you were old enough to play dress up. Your wedding will be BIG in all ways: big dress, big hair, big cake, and big party!

8-11 points: You might be ready to wed, but only if the right guy talks you into it. You're cautious about commitment and protective of your independence. Your bed is pretty cozy as it is, and you'll only make room if the guy is very special.

< 8 points: Wedding schmedding... Who needs it? Not you! You're a lone wolf who's committed to being single above all else. While men are okay, you don't want one around all the time. From what you've seen, they eat too much and sleep too late. Good riddance!

Outerwear

When fur isn't enough…

Quilted comfort

A high collar shields the ears in style while the front zipper adds versatility. The hot pink color means you'll stand out in traffic.

'70s retro ski

Short fur means you need added warmth on chilly days. This sporty throwback to the ski jacket of the 1970s is perfect for cool fall days.

Make a statement

Your mom doesn't zip up your coat anymore!
Share your daring side while still following
mom's advice on staying warm.

fun & distinguished

Opposite: Don't forget to keep your head warm (most body heat is lost from the head) with a fun fleece in hot pink. Above: Nothing is more distinguished than a traditional gray wool overcoat.

poolside pups

Making waves and finding the

perfect suit for your body type!

Opposite: Scooter plays ball in this
floral cover up and yellow daisy lei.

Do you have a broad chest and a tiny lower body?

Then horizontal stripes are perfect for you. Not only do the contrasting horizontal stripes widen a small frame, the off-the-shoulder straps on this pink and cream suit draw attention away from broad shoulders. Additionally, the flouncy skirt gives the illusion of a curvier lower half.

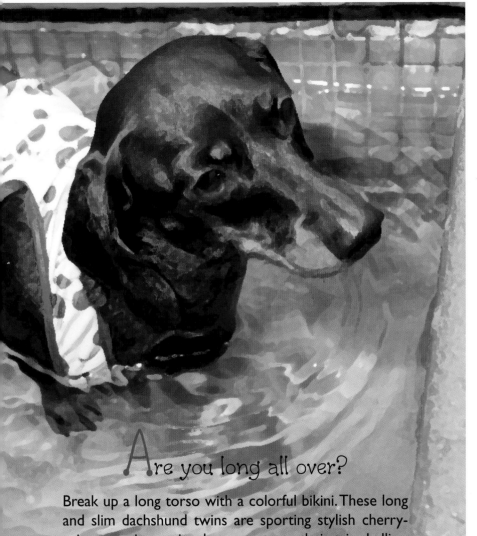

Are you long all over?

Break up a long torso with a colorful bikini. These long and slim dachshund twins are sporting stylish cherry-print two-piece suits that accentuate their trim bellies. Show off!

Are you round all over?

A fashionable and brightly colored skirt can hide all flaws! Unique flower leis around the neck draw the eye to your beautiful face and away from areas where you may have less confidence.

Above: Just because you're round doesn't mean you can't wear bold prints. This fantastic one-piece complements a wide frame while also showing off Shasta's best feature—her adorable tail!

Is your skin sensitive to the sun?

Cover up all over with unique pieces that keep you cool and protected from strong sunlight. This palm print vest, long-sleeve lightweight jersey in orange, and bold, jungle print skirt are a perfect combination for a day in the sun. Don't forget your sunglasses too!

"A chic type, a rough type, an odd type— but never a stereotype."

—Jean-Michel Jarre

What type are you?

Take the quiz on page 80 to find out!

elegant

"Keeping your clothes well pressed will keep you from looking hard pressed."

Coleman Cox

This tasteful mint green and white suit with oversized belt and buckle accent is the picture of elegance. When gracefulness is the goal, tame wispy, wild locks with a simple hair clip that doesn't draw attention to itself.

sophisticated

" I'm interested in longevity,
timelessness, style—not fashion. "

Ralph Lauren

A well-proportioned beret and neck scarf are all
that's needed to achieve a cosmopolitan flare.
The diamond-studded brooch adds a luxurious
touch and ties it all together.

classic

" Fashion fades, style is eternal. "

Yves Saint Laurent

This classic car coat in navy and red with
wooden toggle buttons will never go out of style.
The heavy wool will keep you warm on the
chilliest New England day, while the traditional
design ensures you'll wear it for years to come.

preppy

> "The best thing is to look natural, but it takes makeup to look natural."

Calvin Klein

This back-to-basics pullover sportshirt of knitted cotton achieves a unique look with the multi-colored stripes and the burgundy collar and cuff details. It's just right for a Saturday afternoon of golf, shopping, or lounging in the hammock.

bohemian

> "Luxury must be comfortable;
> otherwise it is not luxury."
>
> Coco Chanel

A carefree spirit can show off in this loose-fitting cotton tunic with botanical print. Lightweight, breathable fabric means you can be stylish without feeling uncomfortable.

tough

Everyone should own a red leather jacket,
especially one with as much attitude as this great
little piece. The quilted stitching and black banding
near the buttons add just enough polish to take
the edge off. The look is completed with a
beaded choker necklace with bone pendant.

wild

> **"** Zest is the secret of all beauty. There is no beauty that is attractive without zest. **"**
>
> Christian Dior

The black T-shirt is a wardrobe staple, especially if it expresses your love of rock-n-roll and punk. Perfect for wearing to a concert, a bar, or an after-bar, this timeless T gets added punch when paired with a light pink choker collar.

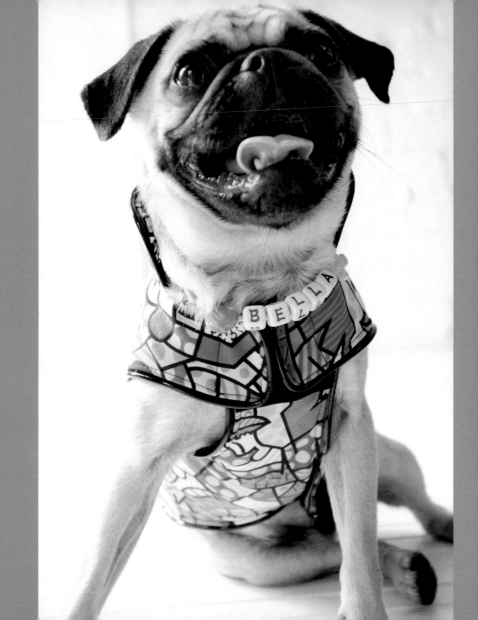

unique

" A woman is never sexier than when
she is comfortable in her clothes. "

Vera Wang

The bold, primary colors of modern art adorn
this one-of-a-kind coverup. The geometric
patterns and black outlining recall the canvases
of Roy Lichtenstein. This artistic look is made
more unique with the signature necklace.

feminine

66 It's about enrapturing yourself in the clothes. 99

Donna Karan

Sometimes, you just can't be too frilly, and this
beautiful party dress is the proof. Pale pink satin
and taffeta make this a special dress for an
important occasion. The matching furry collar and
satin bows at the ears are ideal accents.

individual

Strong personalities deserve equally distinctive clothes, and this velvet jacket in rich tones of red, deep purple, orange, green, and black is just the ticket. The black feathered collar adds playfulness and draws attention to your friendly face.

What type are you?

Take the quiz to find out!

1) On a sunny summer Saturday afternoon, you prefer to:
- A) Catch Frisbees in the park until you're too tired to walk
- B) Take a leisurely stroll through an art fair
- C) Stay on the couch and watch the butterflies float past the front window

2) When riding in the car, you:
- A) Stick your head out the window and bark at all who pass by
- B) Sit quietly but attentively in the passenger seat
- C) Cower in the back seat under your favorite blankie

3) Your favorite place to hang out is:
- A) The beach
- B) Your front yard
- C) Anybody's lap

4) When out with a group of friends, you:
- A) Like to be the center of attention and bark louder than everyone else
- B) Smile a lot and try to be thoughtful of others
- C) Don't have enough friends to call it a "group"

5) When out for a walk and meeting a stranger, you:
- A) Jump up on them and try to lick their face
- B) Tentatively sniff at their shoes
- C) Hide

6) Your style sense can be described as:
- A) Colorful and daring
- B) Trendy and chic
- C) Conservative and simple

Score 3 points for every "A" answer; 2 points for every "B" answer; and 1 point for every "C" answer.

12-18 points: You're definitely a wild one who likes to run with the pack. High energy, outgoing, and flashy are your trademarks. You crave excitement, and can be found howling all night during any full moon.

8-11 points: You prefer early morning strolls to late night soirees. You love head nuzzles, soft petting, and good back scratches on Sunday mornings. You love picnics, long walks, games of catch, and all good, clean American fun.

< 8 points: You're a tender-hearted pooch with a sensitive soul who prefers to watch the world from the sidelines. Your home is your favorite place to be, and you have multiple favorite blankets, stuffed animals, and chew toys. (You also still sleep with your parents.)

Travel Bags

Every dog needs a travel bag, either to carry all of your needed items or to carry... YOU! These one-of-a-kind carryalls can't be matched for usefulness, design or style.

Paris

This exclusive green suede and python pet carrier is the perfect tote if you're heading to Paris. Look smart in a white and black striped shirt with matching beret.

Look ultra-chic while shopping on the streets of Cairo. This pin-dotted suede coat trimmed with animal print goes perfectly with the zebra printed pet carrier.

Africa

Australia

Heading into the bush? This camouflaged outfit of wheat tones and army green will help you blend in with style, while the hot pink animal print pet carrier will make sure you stand out too!

Japan

Asian inspired pieces combine color and elegance with usefulness and durability. The luxurious kimono in bright pinks and yellows is just the complement to the floral print tote-o-pet.

Elaborate botanicals are printed on a rich turquoise field on this "Tokya" coat with gold brocade buttons. The florals on the gold pet carrier pick up these elements, while the coolie finishes the look!

China

Scotland A plaid prep school dress, a beige trench coat, and a herringbone pet carrier are the perfect trio for visiting the British Isles. Don't forget the tea!

England

A mixture of patterns will help you stand out on the London streets. The black in the hat, shirt, and pet carrier unites the separate pieces.

United States

These durable red and blue leather pet carriers are as American as apple pie. The basic, solid colors complement any outfit, while the silver ring details on the strapping add a decorative touch. Any pup would be proud to travel the states in these classic bags.

The following is a list of vendors whose products are featured in this book. Thanks to each of them for their generosity and cooperation. While we have tried to recognize all vendors, we apologize for any omission and, if notified, will gladly add contact information on reprint.

3 Turtle Doves 212-529-3288
The Atlantic Company 401-941-1950
Baby Doll Pliner, 888-307-1630
Barking Baby, barkingbaby.com
Bon Dog, bon-dog.com
Canine Styles, www.caninestyles.com
Cece Cord/Travels with Tiger available through Janet Brown 516-883-2670
Celltei, celltei.com
Charming Pets, charmingpetcharms.com
Chilly Dog, chillydogsweaters.com
Chiwawagaga, chiwawagaga.com, 504-581-4242
Companion Road at petsmart.com
Doggy Design, doggydesign.com
Fancy Furs, fancyfurs.com
Gidget Gear, gidget-gear.com

Haute Diggity Dog, hautediggitydog.com
Little Lily, www.little-lily.com
Nu Breed, nubreeddirect.com
Oliver's Closet, http://oliverscloset.com
Pikala by Jackie Lee, pikalanyc.com
Pink Beans, monkeydaze.com
Posh Pooch, 718-874-6064
Puchi Bag Inc., puchibag.com
Pupcake Studio, pupcakesstudio.com
Puppia, puppiaworld.com
The Ritzy Rover Pet Boutique, theritzyrover.com
The Toby Line, thetobyline.com
Scooter's Friends, scootersfriends.com
Shadow Brown, shadowbrown.com
Sherpa Pet Trading Co., sherpapet.com
Three Dog Bakery 504-525-2253
Louis Vuitton, 866-VUITTON
Wonder Dog, wonderdognyc.com
WOOF, pawpalaceonline.com
Zitomer Z-Spot, zitomer.com